KEEP YOUR PANTS ON

Preventing Infidelity in Your Marriage

Kelly Chisholm MS, LPCC, CRS

Copyright © 2011 Kelly Chisholm. All rights reserved. No portion of this book may be reproduced mechanically, electronically, or by any other means, including photocopying, without written permission of the publisher. It is illegal to copy this book, post it to a website, or distribute it by any other means with- out permission from the publisher.

Kelly Chisholm

Kelly@albuquerquefamilycounseling.com

www.albuquerquefamilycounseling.com

Limits of Liability and Disclaimer of Warranty
The author and publisher shall not be liable for your misuse of this material. This book is strictly for informational and educational purposes.

Warning – Disclaimer

The purpose of this book is to educate and entertain. The author and/or publisher do not guarantee that anyone following these techniques, suggestions, tips, ideas, or strategies will become successful. The author and/or publisher shall have neither liability nor responsibility to anyone with respect to any loss or damage caused, or alleged to be caused, directly or indirectly by the information contained in this book.

ISBN: 978-0-692-95743-1

Acknowledgments

Keep your Pants On would not be possible without many hardworking, dedicated people. The contributions of many valued mentors, trusting couples, and supportive friends and family are so much appreciated!

I am indebted to the couples that have trusted me over the years to help them through extremely difficult times in their relationships. Although therapists receive extensive training, no training is as beneficial or valuable as the training "in the chair." Thank you to all of my clients who have allowed me into their lives to help them weather the storm.

Many special friends gave me encouragement—you know who you are—and thank you to all who were instrumental in getting this book off the ground. Also, my most heartfelt thank you to my family for their unending support, even when I was barely there for them.

For Donna Kozik, who helped me capture my gremlin and lock him away.

For my mom, who supported me on a daily basis with encouragement and an untiring ear.

For my dad, who continually said "Kelly, I always knew you were smart."

And most importantly, for my husband and daughter; without the two of them I would not be where I am today. My deepest love and appreciation goes to you.

Praise for 'Keep Your Pants On'

"Kelly Chisholm doesn't pull any punches. She lays it on the line with real examples of how things can get out of control in a marriage even when people love each other and want their marriage to work. Couples who follow her proactive suggestions throughout the book are sure to avoid devastating threats to their relationship."

Syble Solomon, creator of *Money Habitudes*™

"Kelly Chisholm has written a gem! Based on her professional counseling practice working with couples and research of best practices, she has written a guide for how to avoid an affair. Too late? She also walks the reader through steps to find wholeness if an affair has already taken place. Written in clear, everyday language, Ms. Chisholm incorporates a variety of techniques to keep you turning the pages— case studies, how-tos, conversations to have with your partner, action steps, ideas to ponder… she knows all the tricks and puts them to good use on behalf of the reader. Do yourself and your relationship a favor—read this book!"

Priscilla Hunt, Executive Director, BetterMarriages.org

"This book is an important and timely read for anyone thinking about cheating in their relationships."

Judy Paul

"Take the time to read Ms. Chisholm's book—it will give you insight that will have you thinking about your relationship in a new way."

Bonnie M.

"We had separated and were seriously thinking about divorce—through Kelly's help we were able to transform our relationship into something strong and stable."

Krystle and Tony

"We knew that we were on the brink of something dangerous—this book has helped bring us back from what could have been a disaster."

Peter and Nadine

About the Author

Being in a relationship is hard work these days; the number of break-ups and divorces proves it. The number of relationships that are affected by affairs is staggering, and many relationships and marriages never recover from the complete destruction in trust and confidence. If you are at all involved in current events, it seems that not a day goes by that you don't hear about another marriage or committed relationship that has succumbed to the devastation of an affair.

The problem is that most people don't realize what causes affairs, thinking that their own relationship will be the one and only that is immune from this happening.

Have *you* ever struggled with thoughts of straying from your partner? Have you stayed up at night, alone, while your partner was sleeping, thinking what it would be like to have a different, better, and more exciting relationship with someone else? You'd probably be lying to yourself if you said no. Many people have—and then unfortunately decide to act on the thoughts. This may bring about a fleeting pleasure, a sense of excitement and danger, but most people don't fully realize the consequences of their actions. The ripple effect of their actions has a long arm and a far reach, much to the dismay of the family, friends, and co-workers that are involved.

This is where I come in. What I do is show you how an affair will destroy your relationship, sometimes beyond repair. I help you get really clear about what you want and need in your relationship, to prevent an affair from happening. I provide you with tools and different perspectives to learn about yourself, your vulnerabilities, and how to stay away from trouble areas.

I do this by leading you through a series of action steps that are proven to reduce the influences that can cause an affair.

The reason that I can do this is because for the last ten years I have worked exclusively with couples on the brink—and those that have fallen as well. Through case studies, clinical experience, and a tremendous amount of exposure to the inside world of couple's relationships, I have created a system that works.

To find out more about what every couple should know about preventing affairs, read on and find out my "RSS Feed" (Relationship Secret Strategies) for keeping your pants on.

Contents

Introduction 9
Pain and Pleasure 13
Kodachrome 23
'A' Is for Awareness 29
Love and Fear 35
Environmental Awareness 41
Life Transitions 49
'N' Is for Needs 53
Motorcycle Mama 57
For Women Only 63
'T' Is for Trust 67
Social Calls 73
Scuba Lessons 77
'S' Is for SMART Goals 83
The 5Cs Reconnection Plan 89
Healthy Habits 99
Now What? 103
If All Else Fails 107
The Price of Forgiveness 115

Introduction

It's 2:15 on a Thursday afternoon, and I am sitting in my office. I am the founder of a private counseling practice that is focused on couples and their relationships. On this day, a man and a woman are sitting with me, in separate chairs. Their body language is telling: They lean away from each other, arms and legs crossed, stiff expressions on their faces. The sadness and hurt coming from this couple are filling the room, like a huge wave of emotion that thickens the air itself. The woman is sobbing, her tears becoming large rivulets that run down her face and smear her make-up. Her husband offers her a tissue, but she waves it away, completely turning her body away from his in total rejection. He starts to talk to her, trying to find words to explain something that he has tried to explain countless times before today.

I am in therapist mode, listening to the couple tell their story about the husband's infidelity. This is certainly not the first time that I have heard this story; I've heard it literally from hundreds of couples before this one. It's not always the man who is the cheater; infidelity is now equal-opportunity for men and women. But today it is the man, his wife joining the ranks of the betrayed by discovering evidence of an affair. They have come to me for guidance, for support, and to help them navigate the choppy waters of repairing their marriage. The woman is not at all certain that she even wants to repair the marriage, and that will be the first phase of counseling as we search for clarity.

I sit there with this couple, sharing their pain. This is what therapists do: We sit with the client's pain, and sometimes we are the only other person that the client has who can or will sit with that pain. What is going through my mind is this: Why can't I stop this pain from happening? I know so much about repairing an affair, having helped hundreds of couples through this. If I could just get to these couples *before* an affair, could I make a difference? Is there something that I could do that would prevent even one person from having an affair?

If stopping the pain of an affair was something that I could impact, and then I needed to put everything that I have learned over the years into some action steps that could steer a person out of the path of an oncoming affair. If the tools and strategies that work in my office could benefit another couple's relationship before it was too late, then it needed to be available to everyone. And so, this book was born.

Getting the Most from This Book

This is not the typical book on preventing affairs. Many of the books already published are focused on how to keep your partner happy so that he or she won't have any desire to stray outside of the relation-ship. That's great in theory, but not in practice. Most people who have had affairs will freely admit that his or her partner had nothing to do with the choice in having an affair. Choosing to have an affair comes from the *individual* person, not because of the partner or anyone else. The choice of an affair is wrongly made because of very specific motivations, environments, and behaviors that went unchecked for a long time—long enough for some self-delusion and denial to take place. This book intends to show you how to stop yourself from having an affair—before it's too late.

Since you're reading this book, you must be interested in what helps to keep your pants on. This book has several components, all designed to give you quick, relatively easy steps to get on track with preventing an affair.

- **Action Steps:** developed to work both individually or as a couple.
- **Case Studies:** to be used as personal assessments. Ask yourself "Could this be me?"
- **RSS Feeds:** quick tips of reflection and self-review.

Pain and Pleasure

"An hour of pain is as long as a day of pleasure."
~ *Unknown*

Many people who have had affairs look back and say "I don't know what made me do this. I don't understand what I was feeling at the time." It's true that our actions and behaviors always seem different when we look at them in the rear-view mirror, and it's important to know why we do the things that we do. One of the first things that we can do to prevent affairs is to understand what motivates our own behavior and actions.If we understand these ideas, we are better prepared to can handle our emotions. Knowing and being aware of our emotions *before* we find ourselves in a compromised state is crucial to our healthy relationships. How do we know what drives us, motivates us, and causes us to make the choices that we do?

Most people are driven by one of two things: pain or pleasure. People are motivated to get away from the pain, or move toward the pleasure. If you think about every decision that you make, everything boils down to avoidance of pain or a desire for pleasure. Let's take a closer look at this principle.

First, let's look at the word *pain*. We typically think of pain as a physical condition, but it also has different meanings to each of us based on our past experiences. For some people, pain can also mean discomfort, boredom, loss, fear, or grief. As we pull from our past experiences, we label the emotion "pain," only knowing that it is a feeling that we want to avoid experiencing again at all costs. So, when we subconsciously think about pain it can actually be a different emotion, but our experience tells us that we have a negative association with the emotion and want to avoid it.

Here's an example. Ask yourself "What keeps me from sitting down and trying to communicate with my partner?" We can usually answer this with "I know that if I bring up anything to my partner about our relationship, it will just start a fight." You are trying to avoid the discomfort (pain) of your past experiences—when you have argued with your partner, the emotional yelling, and the feeling of being unloved, disconnected, and the dreaded silences afterward.

Sometimes you avoid the pain based on another life experience besides the current environment, remembering other times in your life that an argument felt terrible. Dredging up the time when you argued with your father about money for college may bring up more unpleasant sensations about arguing, leaving you with the emotional equivalent of "arguing equals pain."

Of course, every individual will experience pain and pleasure differently. Let's say your partner asks you to attend an important social function with him or her this weekend. Will you go? Would this be pleasure or pain? It would depend on the meaning that you associate with socializing. People who are outgoing and enjoy social gatherings might see it as pleasurable: an opportunity to meet new people, engage in small talk, and have fun with your partner. For others, having to engage in conversation with strangers is equal to slow torture. These people would have a strong association of pain with the social event, considering going would be an excruciating endeavor to be avoided at all costs. Even some people who would normally find pleasure in the social event might decide not to go. Maybe they perceive the pleasure of going to the event to be less than the pleasure of spending alone time with their partner. Is the pain of going to this function greater or less than the pain of your disappointed partner? Or is the pleasure of your excited, happy partner greater than your own pain if you attend?

On a daily basis, we go through this emotional balancing act and make our decisions based on the avoidance of pain and pursuit of pleasure. We continually weigh our possible options and choose actions based on our personal associations of pain and pleasure. Our choices, motivated by these polarized principles, affect our lives, and our actions have consequences that mirror our choices. Understanding what motivates you instantly affects your choices and their outcomes.

How does this affect our motivations, decisions, and choices about affairs?

We all have common levels of pain avoidance, founded on our basic needs. Avoiding pain in a relationship often looks like this:

- Feelings of anger or resentment toward your partner, manifesting in loss of affection, intimacy or attraction
- Feelings of being misunderstood or disconnected from partner
- Feelings of being alone or rejected
- Numbness, boredom, and apathy
- A feeling of being undesirable, unappreciated, or undervalued

These sentiments are commonly reported among those who have had affairs. Partners who are feeling too much of any of the above are looking for **something to take away the pain.** The emotional pull toward an affair is based on avoidance of these states of pain.

What about the pursuit of pleasure? We subscribe to the notion that an affair is always about the pursuit of pleasure, but the fact is that we are re-ally more hard-wired to avoid pain than to gain pleasure. This means that we will usually choose actions that will avoid pain, not those that pursue pleasurable states. Gaining pleasure would seem to be an enormous motivation toward having an affair, but choosing to have an affair is typically a response to avoiding your own pain. Here are some descriptions of the pleasure factor that led many to the path of an affair:

- Wanting some excitement, something "new"
- Wanting to feel needed, appreciated, desired, and attractive
- Sexual excitement or uniqueness
- Having the opportunity to "be" somebody different, step out of his or her role, or try on a new "hat"

As you can see in comparing the two lists above, gaining pleasure is often a direct response to avoiding the current pain of the relationship. If you are feeling rejected, unwanted, or undesirable, you will look outside of the relationship to avoid those painful feelings.

The fear of loss is another feeling that overrides desire for pleasure. Most people are more interested in keeping what they have than in taking a risk to gain more. What are the guaranteed losses that you will experience if you decide to have an affair? Affairs will cause you to lose:

- All sense of safety in your relationship
- All of your privacy
- Your sense of self and self-esteem (and your partner's)
- Innocence
- All sense of normalcy and functioning
- The respect of your partner, children, family, and friends; and, most importantly, your own self-respect
- The commitment of your relationship

These are the most common losses among people who have had affairs, and this list is not complete.

Here is your guarantee: **By beginning an affair, you are 100% guaran-teed to feel more pain than the pleasure you might have felt about the affair.** People who have had affairs continually report that they "had no idea what kind of pain" they would feel. If you have not had an affair (and I hope you have not) you need to know the amount of pain that will be caused to you, your partner, children, family, friends, and professional contacts.

The fleeting pleasure of the affair is *always* defeated by the pain that comes in ongoing, steadily increasing waves. This is one area of our lives where time does not heal all. The consequences of an affair are far-reaching and time-resistant; think of them as a ripple effect that lasts an excruciatingly long time.

How do we use this knowledge and awareness to prevent an affair? The answer is this: **We need to mentally link enough pain to having an affair**

and enough pleasure to being faithful. Can we learn to associate the actions of having an affair with pain and those of being faithful to pleasure? First, we need to know how to link the concepts of "pain" and "affair" together. This will produce a mindset that will continually cue us that the large amount of pain that comes from having an affair is not worth the small amount of pleasure it will give us. If we link extreme amounts of pain to any behavior, we will avoid it at all costs. There are two ways to create a link to what equals pain: experiencing it yourself, or being shown by others what the consequences are of that action. When applying this concept to the potential of having an affair, experiencing it is actually living through the pain, an action we are trying to avoid. So, the only answer left is to be shown what the consequences would be of having an affair.

Visualizations can help you make that association. Visualizations are scenes that we play over in our heads based on our realities, or what our minds might be imagining. A good visualization includes using all your senses, and can challenge the ideas and beliefs that we have, breaking through the illusions and projections that we have surrounding affairs. When reading through the following scenes, try imagining them with your sense of touch, sight, smell, taste, and hearing.

Imagine the following scenes in your head:

1. You have been having an affair with a co-worker for several months, and you find out that your affair partner's wife has had you both followed by a private investigator. The investigator has pictures, tapes, and records that show all your illicit meetings. Your affair partner's wife is going to your spouse with all the evidence. You feel like you have been kicked in the stomach and the world has fallen out from beneath you. How do you handle this with your husband? How do you go back into work the next day, the next week, the next month?

2. Your adult child wants to get married. He or she comes to you and wants to know why you got divorced and what really happened in your marriage. How will you answer this question? What advice will you give your child? Will you tell him or her the truth—that you had an affair and the marriage fell apart? How will this affect your relationship with your child? How will your child see you now? What lasting effect will this new knowledge have on his or her own marriage?

3. You have left your relationship for your affair partner. It's Christmas, and when you call your ex to speak with the kids, a strange man answers the phone. How do you feel about the prospect of having someone else raising your children? What will it be like for you to call to talk with your kids and have someone with an attitude answer the phone? How will you feel about not having your children with you for every holiday? How will you feel about your children sharing their time with another step-family?

These scenes are based on reality; they are true reports from those who have had affairs. There is nothing pleasurable about the outcomes. Dealing with your ex-partner's new love and having him or her fulfill a parenting role with your own children is a given, as over time your ex-partner will certainly move into another relationship. Having to tell your adult children how and what you did in having an affair—explaining why your marriage ended—is not going to enhance your relationship with your kids.

Going into work and having to face the affair partner after an affair with a co-worker has been discovered is very awkward, uncomfortable, and humiliating. When the affair is with a co-worker, the place of structure and routine that should be the office is now a place of shame and humiliation. Can you afford to get another job quickly, to avoid the pain? Most people cannot, and the higher you are in your career, the harder it will be to leave. The years of personal achievement for which you have worked hard are now hanging by a thread based on your actions. Many people who have had affairs with co-worker's experience this as a huge amount of pain. Not only do they have to deal with the pain at home with their spouse, but also at their workplace. This provides a never-ending painful environment from which there is no relief and no getting away from. Can you think of anything more miserable than an atmosphere of non-stop pain?

Here's another idea to help you make that mental link of pain with having an affair:

> Make a "loss" list. Spend 15 minutes and write down everything that you might lose or that you will certainly lose by having an affair. Think about how your environment, and your sense of safety and normalcy will change. List *all* the people who will be affected by your affair—not just your partner. Consider the "ripple effect" of the affair (friends, family, co-workers who will be affected).
>
> When you are finished with your list, re-read it. The potential losses can be staggering, and that's what you need to know.

RSS Feed:
Pain has a very loud voice. Pay attention to what it is saying.

People who have affairs almost never intend to leave their partner. People who engage in affairs are just like you and me. They are looking for something that they perceive not to be present in the current relationship, but they really have no thought or intent of leaving their spouse. The reality is that many relationships do not survive an affair, and that the betrayed partner may never get over the destruction and pain caused by the crumbled foundation of the relationship.

Now that we know how to link pain and affair, we need to make a link to what equals pleasure: being faithful. Let's look at the meaning of the word *fidelity*. Loyalty, dependability, devotion, commitment, reliability, and trustworthiness are all elements of the idea of fidelity. Thousands of couples get married every year; do they want a different version of fidelity than commitment and devotion? What are your expectations and beliefs regarding fidelity in a relationship? The truth is, does anyone really gets married that has a different meaning of the word? Ask yourself what your own personal beliefs are about:

- Commitment
- Relationship
- Marriage
- Trust

What meanings do you associate with these words? I can say without reservation that *nobody* marries because they want a "sometimes" commitment, trust only on his or her terms, or wants a relationship only when it suits him or her.

Kodachrome

"The truth is that we can learn to condition our minds, bodies and emotions to link pain or pleasure to whatever we choose. By changing what we link pain and pleasure to, we will instantly change our behaviors."

~ Tony Robbins

Let's look at a couple who ran from their pain right into the path of an affair.

Greg and Kathy had been married over 25 years when they came to marriage counseling. They had raised a family together, had long and fulfilling professional careers, and were financially comfortable. Kathy had just discovered that Greg had been having an affair with another woman for the past two years, and they both were motivated to understand what had happened in their once-stable relationship. In the beginning sessions, the pain of the affair took over the room, with both partners experiencing the full impact of the consequences of what had happened. But the story was not just about the affair; there were other issues going on. Through many tears and emotions, they told their deeper story about one of their children, who had been the victim of a violent crime. The crime went unsolved, and the family was in tremendous pain over the injustice of the legal system that they had formerly trusted. All attempts to rectify the situation and gain a sense of fairness and balance had been denied. As a result, the family splintered apart, with each family member taking their pain and isolating themselves from each other. This had happened two years earlier, around the time that Greg began his affair.

This couple had several challenges to overcome: a complete breakdown of trust, feelings of guilt and blame, a lack of emotional intimacy. When a family is in crisis, they need tremendous emotional support. This family received none; they were let down by the legal system, professionals, their friends, and external family members. Greg and Kathy believed that they were handling the situation as best they could, by circling the wagons and protecting what was left in their crumbling family structure. They were strong people and felt that they could weather the storm alone. Most heartbreaking of all, as they looked to each other for emotional support, neither one could fully be there for the other partner.

From the pain caused by his child's victimization, from his own overwhelming emotions, from his sense of isolation from Kathy, and from his feeling of powerlessness over the situation, Greg had run straight into an affair. This couple needed my help to sort through the events that had happened and identify the "activating event" of the affair: the violent crime that had occurred in their family. This incident pushed all their existing support and stability to the breaking point, and caused isolation and loneliness between the two of them, compounded by feelings of guilt and blame.

Our solution to the problem was to first realize what had led to the affair, the emotional states that were present, and to answer the painful questions that Greg and Kathy had refused to recognize. The couple needed a Kodachrome "snapshot" of the events surrounding the affair, to identify where the pain really was coming from and how the affair began. With much inner work and some very painful conversations, they realized that they had not been there for each other in a time of severe need, that they both had blamed the other for what had happened, and that they did the exact opposite of what they should have done (be present, support, and help each other to get through the extremely challenging time). Greg had run into the arms of another woman to try to relieve the intense pain that he was feeling—a pain that would truly be alleviated only by his wife's support. Kathy tried to bury her own emotions by completely distancing herself from Greg. Her pain was internal, as she blamed herself for the incident.

The result of the counseling was that Kathy and Greg had a new aware-ness of and empathy about what each other had gone through. Through my guidance, Kathy and Greg slowly rebuilt the foundation of their marriage by facing the pain that they had experienced, answering the difficult questions for each other and using the action steps at the back of this book.

Being aware of the pain/pleasure concept had a tremendous effect on the outcome of this couple. As of the writing of this book, Greg and Kathy are still together and agree that they are building a stronger marriage than they ever had before.

If this were your situation, what would you do? What would you want your partner to know about your pain? What would you want your partner to do in a crisis? How would you and your partner get through an issue that was bigger than the two of you? Asking yourself these questions can help you prevent actions that are consequences of the pain and pleasure principle.

RSS Feed:

Find your personal pain and pleasure links, and be aware of your pressure gauge. Understand what the true pain and pleasure is regarding an affair. Knowledge and awareness of these two principles will keep you on course.

'A' Is for Awareness

What does awareness look like when trying to prevent an affair? Being alert to your own emotions, observant with your partner's emotions, and consistent with your efforts to understand those emotions constitutes awareness.

RSS Feed:
Self-awareness, combined with environmental awareness, is crucial to preventing affairs in your relationships.

In preventing affairs, awareness relates to two themes: awareness of one's own emotional levels, and awareness of the vulnerable states and environments that can intensify the desire for an affair. In case studies, research, and surveys, the number-one reason that people give for their infidelities is emotional dissatisfaction in the relationship. Why are so many people disconnected emotionally from their partners, to the point that they choosing the risky behavior of having an affair? Let's first look at how we can identify our own emotional levels and how they can become out of balance.

Really, what is the big deal about being aware of our emotions? Most people believe that they are in control of their emotions, when it is really the other way around. We can learn to manage our emotions, but not before we are aware of what they are.

We start identifying our emotions early in childhood, labeled with the few terms that we hear most often: happy, sad, angry, or afraid. As adults, we don't go much beyond this small list, adding envy, boredom, and loneliness to our bag of feelings. Sometimes these labels don't accurately describe our true feelings, and we become frustrated with our inability to communicate with our partners or ourselves. For many people, being able to verbally communicate their feelings with their partner is the truest form of intimacy. In crisis, one of the first things that couples say is that they can't communicate.

How is it possible to communicate when you don't have the awareness of your own emotions?

RSS Feed:
Our emotions are the most reliable indicators of how things are going on in our relationships.

Some people disregard their emotions because they feel they are too much trouble to keep in check, or too painful to bring out. Emotions rule our thoughts and actions, so not paying attention to them is comparable to postponing dinner when you are ravenous. We all know what happens when you ignore your hunger: At the next opportunity for food, you will overeat to the point of being uncomfortable. Just like your hunger, emotions can come back at inconvenient times and control your actions if you are not aware of what is going on within yourself. Out-of-control actions are at the root of affairs; those emotions that you have been ignoring burst out of you at the most vulnerable times, leading you toward a choice that has a path of pain and chaos.

RSS Feed:
Repeatedly, people who have had an affair will describe it as "it just happened," "I fell into it," "I didn't know what I was doing," and "I wasn't myself."

Being aware of your emotions is critical not only to your own personal well-being and happiness, but to your relationship and inclination toward having an affair. In preventing an affair in your relationship, the math is easy: $A+B=C$.

If you are:

    A) Not in tune to what you are feeling, or

    B) Suppressing or burying your emotions, then

C) You don't know what's lurking beneath the surface of your consciousness, **leaving your emotions totally in control of your actions.**

Not being aware of your own emotions may explain some of the thoughtless actions, but it does not excuse the actions.

Love and Fear

"Power is of two kinds, love and fear. Power based on love is a thousand times more effective and permanent than power based on fear."

~ *Gandhi*

We all have two fundamental emotions that we experience: love and fear. Other emotions are variations of these two emotions, which drive our thoughts and behavior. From these emotions, our choices and actions come from either a place of love or a place of fear. Anxiety, anger, control, sadness, depression, inadequacy, confusion, hurt, loneliness, guilt, shame—these are all fear-based emotions. Joy, happiness, caring, trust, compassion, truth, contentment, satisfaction—these are love-based emotions.

There are varying degrees of intensity of both types of emotions, some mild, others moderate, and still others strong in intensity. For example, anger in a mild form can be felt as disgust or dismay, at a moderate level can be felt as offense or exasperation, and at an intense level can be felt as rage or hate. The emotion that always underpins anger is fear.

RSS Feed:

An awareness that can immediately change our lives and relationships is the understanding that we make all our choices based on either fear or love.

Ask yourself the following questions: In choosing to have an affair, am I deciding based on fear or love? Am I running from a fear of intimacy with my partner and choosing to have a superficial fling to calm that inner fear? Am I letting a fear of abandonment push me in a direction with consequences that I will not be able to ignore?

People's most primal fear is not being accepted and loved. If you are responding to your emotional dissatisfaction in your primary relationship by turning or running away toward an affair, these actions would come from a fear-based perspective.

Here's an example of a love-based action:

> You are contemplating having an affair. Say to yourself "This is a relationship that I chose. I made a commitment to myself and my partner, and my choices have consequences. I care enough for myself, my integrity, my values, and my partner to choose an action that is based on love. That action would be to tell my partner how I am feeling, and have an honest conversation as to what we can do about my feelings."

Sometimes we suppress emotions because they are too painful to deal with, or we do not understand or recognize what emotions we are feeling. Suppressed emotions within a relationship cause your behavior and reactions to events in the present moment to really be reactions to past events. This has a negative effect on all relationships in your life. It's hard to be in the present with your partner, to *really* see what he or she is doing and saying when you are thinking about past hurts and resentments. We bury emotions because we feel that they are painful and difficult to deal with. Since you are the one that creates your own emotions, you can also be the one to change them.

It takes a lot of energy to bury emotions and to keep them buried. There isn't much energy left for other activities when your energy is being used to keep stuffing these emotions back down.

Here are five indicators that you might be bottling your emotions within your relationship:

- Rarely talking about your feelings
- Focusing discussions on children or work instead of talking about the relationship
- Blowing up over minor incidents
- Boredom, apathy, or discomfort

- Excessive or compulsive behaviors in eating, working, exercising, sex, or drug/alcohol use

Trying to deny your emotions is not the solution, and understanding and using them are good tools to prevent an affair. Think of your emotions as an internal compass, guiding you in the direction that you want to go. But where is the instruction sheet for the compass? If you were going hiking, would you go without knowing how to get home if you got lost? The compass would be use the single most important piece of equipment you would take with you. If you don't know how to use the compass, it will lead you astray with any small wind that blows your way. So, how do we give ourselves a reality check about emotions? It takes time, attention, and consistency, but the payoff is worthwhile.

"Let's not forget that the little emotions are the great captains of our lives and we obey them without realizing it."

~ Vincent Van Gogh

Here are some ideas to begin managing your emotions before they manage you:

- Identify what you are really feeling. Instead of feeling overwhelmed, step back for a minute and ask yourself "What am I *really* feeling right now? Am I really feeling angry, or is it more hurt or sorrow? Maybe I feel like I have lost something, and that is the stronger feeling. What's that all about?"
- Acknowledge your emotions, and realize that they are a healthy part of you. Anger is one emotion that gets a bad rap, but it's only the *actions* of anger that can be negative, not the emotion itself.
- After recognizing the emotion and realizing that the emotion itself is not a terrible thing, try to remember another time that you had this emotion. How did you deal with it then? Knowing

that you dealt with an emotion in the past (and you did) gives you the confidence to handle it again. This takes away the fear of having the emotion, and enables you to feel successful about your efforts.

Once you have begun to manage your emotions, find a technique to release any that are getting in the way of your relationship. This can be done in a number of ways: talking, journaling, prayer, personal reflection, or professionally through counseling. Above all, accept responsibility for your emotions and don't be afraid of them. Remember: We make our choices based on either fear or love, so be powerful and make yours out of love.

Environmental Awareness

We've talked a lot about emotional awareness and how to recognize the signs of trouble within ourselves and our relationships. Let's address our physical environments as a potential threat for affairs. As individuals, we can find ourselves in some pretty sticky positions sometimes— situations that, logically, we *never* intended to be in. We also have some vulnerability factors—those aspects of our environment and our character that that raise the risk of having an affair. Knowing about these ahead of time can help prevent us from falling down our emotional rabbit hole, which may end up as an affair.

- Physical environments
- Transitions of life
- Personal belief system, family history, and internal messages.

Physical Environments

Our minds barely register the numerous accounts that we have heard about a celebrity or sports figure divorcing due to an affair. Members of some industries and professions are more inclined to have affairs, due in part to the high state of emotional arousal that is involved. It is well-documented that settings that have a high "drama quotient" (such as entertainment, law enforcement, emergency, or military personnel) have a higher incidence of affairs.

Corporate and office environments are another huge source of affairs, another well-known fact. Who doesn't know of at least one person who has been burned by an office romance? When we spend more waking hours at the office, conferencing, traveling, or in meetings than we do with our primary partner, it's not difficult to see how office love can bloom frequently and readily.

Have you ever had a relationship with a co-worker that felt more comfortable than your relationship with your partner? Many people can answer that question affirmatively. Why is that? Look at warning signs that may indicate a "Danger: Upcoming Emotional Rabbit Hole" about your opposite-sex co-worker:

- Saving certain jokes, stories, or conversations for use only at the office, instead of sharing them with your mate
- Finding yourself looking forward to seeing and interacting with this person when you go to work, and/or thinking of him or her in a context other than the daily business dynamics that would normally occur
- Realizing that the content of your conversations with your co-worker contains sexual overtones, venting about your intimate relationship, or other personal details of your life
- Using your co-worker as a sounding board for ideas or topics that should be only for your partner

If any of these sounds like you, then really look at your motivations. Are you running from pain or walking toward pleasure? Have a good conversation with yourself, find out what the impulse is behind this work relationship, and crush it before it takes flight in a direction that you never intended.

Let's face it, we all go to work in some capacity, and it's not possible to change our work environments at the drop of a hat. Keep the workplace for work, not romantic experimentation.

> **"A long marriage is two people trying to dance a duet and two solos at the same time."**
> *~ Anne Fleming*

Here's another perspective on work and marriage. In *The E-myth Revisited*, Michael Gerber discusses at length his idea of the difference between working *on* your business versus working *in* your business. The basic premise is that when you work too much *in* the business, you can't effectively work *on* the business, and that severely restricts the long-term success of the business. Because of you putting too much focus on the application, the bigger picture went unattended and consequently failed.

If we apply this standard to a relationship, what is the difference between working *in* the relationship and working *on* the relationship? As a society, we are really good at working *in* a relationship. We go through our days of overscheduled, overcommitted lives, just to come home, collapse for a few hours, and start the same pattern over again the next day. Many couples have two careers and are masters at juggling their professional schedules, navigating their corporate environments, and racing their way up the corporate ladder. Couples compete to "out-earn" each other, accept higher responsibilities within their jobs, and still volunteer to coach the soccer team. Both men and women want their own identities that are separate from the household and their own individual successes. The American work ethic is alive and kicking, as we continually demonstrate by our neglect of our relationships.

How do we compare working *on* the relationship? If the current divorce data are any indication, not well. Working on the relationship takes time and effort, but, more importantly, consistency. Let's compare this idea of consistency to losing weight, something most of us have all tried to do at some point in our lives.

How many times have you tried to do the necessary things to lose weight—cut back on calories, exercise more, or make more healthy choices—just to be frustrated by the efforts? Making the choice to give up just one cookie does not get you to your ideal weight, but making that choice many times over the course of a month will. Consistency and continuity are the keys to losing weight—or working on a relationship. Small, baby steps of being consistent in your actions, behaviors, and thoughts toward your partner are the key to a lasting and healthy relationship.

We see many celebrity couples split. Knowing your partner inside and out, sometimes for many years, is not enough to keep the relationship together. These celebrity couples certainly spent a lot of time working *in* their relationships, but not *on* them. Consistent and continual effort must be made and the big picture of the relationship attended to, by both partners at the same time. Your partner's love, affection, and respect will not wait while you work in the relationship.

Technology

What is the single most threatening thing to your relationship today? I'll give you a hint: It's smaller than a breadbox, is more powerful than an atomic bomb, and can travel the universe in nano-seconds, and you have one in your pocket right now. So, take out your cell phone from your pocket and give it to your partner, let him or her have it for an hour, and be secure in the knowledge that **there is nothing on that cell phone that you don't want him or her to see.**

What? Is there some resistance there? Have you been surfing, texting, or talking to someone or something that your partner may not like? If you have videos, photos, websites, or texts on your phone that you would not want your significant other to see, that should be a wake-up call. Maybe it's time to set the alarm.

When looking at environmental influences that can push you into an affair, the threats of technology to our relationships cannot be ignored. While the internet, social media, texting, and e-mail can be benefits to your relationship, more often they become weapons of mass destruction. We've all heard about the thousands of text messages discovered that were sent to an affair partner, the "sexting" that happens frequently, and the social media sites that promote relationships with someone other than your own partner. Yet, more time is spent on the internet and cell phones than face to face with our partners, and then we wonder why the relationship feels as dry and stale as an old crust of bread. Here's a quick list of do's and don'ts when it comes to technology, relationships, and preventing an affair:

- DON'T get into a predicament with an old flame on Facebook or Classmates. Be open with your communications and let your partner know who you are "friending."
- DON'T use technology as a shield or replacement for your feelings. Texting how you feel is not the same as speaking it.
- DON'T use technology to be emotionally disconnected from your partner or to connect artificially with someone else.
- DO use the cell phone or text as an instant connection with your partner a few times each day with a friendly message or just to say, "I'm thinking about you."
- DO use technology to your mutual benefit, by checking out information from which you can both benefit. What can technology do for you as a couple? Reviews of movies and books, real estate listings, medical information—the list goes on. Make it work *for* you, not *against* you.
- DO have some agreed-on limitations for your tech usage with you partner, like setting up a tech-free zone in the house or tech-free times of the day.

RSS Feed:
Technology can either be a great gift or a painful backstab. It's your choice, so make it work for your relationship, not against it.

Life Transitions

Life changes such as relocations, parenthood, deaths, and job changes affect our emotional states, in turn affecting our decisions to engage in an affair. The stresses of our lives can cause a tremendous upheaval of our emotions. Any change in the status quo can throw our emotions into a vulnerable state. Positive changes such as becoming a parent are also stressors, and the inability to recognize our emotions around these situations can set us up for relationship failure.

The Perfect Storm

Rob was just about to turn 40, had achieved a high status in his chosen career, and had a loving, strong relationship with his wife, Diana. They had been married for several years and had talked about having a child, but when Diana announced that she was pregnant, Rob felt like his world just dropped. The perfect storm of emotions occurred: The impact of getting older, the additional responsibility that comes with parenthood, and his feeling that the best days of his career were behind him knocked him off balance before he even realized what was happening. The emotional swamp he found himself in led to a damaging path of an affair with a younger woman at work. Rob was always very tied into his career identity, and felt that he was in danger of losing that identity in becoming a father. He wasn't emotionally ready for that transition, and with the added stress of turning 40, he succumbed to his emotional need of feeling "younger," by getting involved with someone who fed that need.

At the time, Rob was not mentally prepared to be a father, but he knew his wife really wanted to have a child. Thinking about becoming a father was a role that he was not comfortable with, and a shift in his identity that he was not prepared to make. The affair partner at work saw him as an attractive, upwardly mobile professional with many achievements in his field.

It boosted his self-esteem that a younger woman would find him attractive, and fed into his existing identity. In addition, every time he came home, he felt that his wife's attention went to the new baby and not him. Though he understood with his head that this attention was a necessary part of becoming new parents, what he didn't fully realize was how it was making his heart feel neglected and lonely. Looking back, Rob realized that he was caught in a whirlwind of emotions and was unable to sort through them until the dust cleared, and the affair was exposed.

What was going on with Rob and Diana was that Rob had succumbed to a combination of life transitions, let his emotions lead him, and consequently chose the wrong path. By turning 40, becoming a father, and feeling that his identity was at risk, the perfect storm of emotions was created. Rob knew that he had let these subconscious emotions take over his mind, causing actions that he deeply regretted. Becoming more aware of his own feelings about his life, his marriage, and his family was essential to preventing even more pain.

Many sessions were devoted to the examination of Rob's emotions—and to Diana's as she witnessed the breakdown of their marriage. The aware-ness of Rob's perfect storm of emotions was a great healing tool for Rob and Diana as they worked through the confusion that their lives had be-come. Today, they are stronger as a couple, and they know that they will never be in the same emotional environment that caused the affair because of their new awareness as a couple and as individuals.

RSS Feed:
Don't sit on the stool without three legs or you will fall. Communication, awareness, and choice are the legs that will hold you up.

'N' Is for Needs

"They say a person needs just three things to be truly happy in the world: someone to love, something to do and something to hope for."

~ *Tom Burdett*

Everyone has needs, from the most basic needs of food and shelter to the higher needs of personal growth and fulfillment. When our needs are not met, we find ourselves frustrated and unhappy. One large problem that comes up in relationships is that the need for "self" sometimes interferes with the needs of the couple.

Many of us have the basic needs met, but what about the others? When was the last time you spent some time identifying what your own needs were, or those of your partner? Both men and women have a need for "self" within the relationship along with the need for intimacy. As an individual prior to being in your relationship, you were an appealing person with unique interests and opinions. In forming a relationship, many times that individual is buried within the need for closeness or becoming a couple. This need for self should be stated loud and clear; putting aside your own needs for the sake of someone else is a nice gesture, but the feeling you gain will be short-term. Balance is the key: having your needs met as well as your partner's—and realizing that neither one of you can possibly meet all the needs of the other.

RSS Feed:

If you stop growing either within a relationship or as an individual, you will dry up and die.

Motorcycle Mama

Brenda and Tim had been married for ten years, had flourishing professional lives and careers, and had started their relationship with a solid foundation of mutual respect and caring. They had no children, deciding instead to put their time and energy into their respective careers. In the beginning, they were mutually supportive of the long hours and traveling that was a weekly part of their jobs. But after ten years, Brenda felt completely disconnected from Tim and saw the current relationship as being more like roommates than lovers under the same roof. One morning Brenda had a wake-up call when she found a text from Tim to a co-worker that seemed inappropriate. After she confronted Tim, he agreed that he and Brenda had lost their connection and were unable to even hold an engaging conversation together. They discussed the lack of emotional intimacy, sexual intimacy, and excitement that they felt toward each other. Brenda and Tim both confessed to having thoughts of straying outside of the marriage to feel loved and desired again, thinking that their partner had completely lost interest in them and their relationship.

This couple had several issues that needed to be addressed, and needs that were going unfulfilled. In the early stages of their relationship, Brenda and Tim had put every ounce of their energy into their careers and professions, which they both agreed that they wanted to do. The results were that they had thriving, demanding careers that they loved, but had let the relationship stagnate to the point of starvation. At night when they came home, it was a quick dinner together while discussing the day's work activities, then right back to the computer and phone to finish up for the day. This left little time for themselves or the relationship, and after years of neglect the relationship was withering away on the vine. Their individual needs of affection, companionship, and physical touch were completely unmet, making their relationship ripe for an affair.

When Brenda and Tim came into my office for the first time, they looked pretty weary. They were relieved that neither one had entered an affair, but were saddened at how close they had come to doing just that. We worked together on their unmet needs, both as a couple and as individuals. What developed was a new understanding of themselves, of each other, and of what their ideas would be for the relationship moving forward.

This is the process that we used—with spectacular results. I helped them identify and communicate their needs to each other, focusing on the physical touch (Brenda's need) and the need for excitement and newness (Tim's need). These two needs were the most primary, as identified by the couple. Other needs that were considered were Tim's need to not have to talk about things all the time, and Brenda's need for routine and structure. Combining these identified needs, their homework assignment to find an activity that they would both enjoy and that they would willingly do together. The result was this: After researching and discussing together what they wanted, Brenda and Tim bought a motorcycle together. They now take trips every Friday and Saturday evening after work. This was a great result that satisfied all their needs:

- Tim's need for excitement and newness
- Brenda's need for physical touch (She must hang on Tim's back for long periods of time!)
- Tim's need for "quiet time," (not having to talk while riding the cycle)
- Brenda's need for routine and structure (having a schedule that they could count on a weekly basis)
- Most importantly, their combined need of spending some quality time together so that they could re-connect

Action Step

All human beings have emotional needs that they want to be fulfilled. When these needs are not satisfied, we feel sad, depressed, lonely, hurt, disappointed, or even worthless. To help you identify and specify which of your needs are unmet, look through this list. Too often, people rely on others or life's circumstances to get their needs met, only to be disappointed. A healthier approach is to do everything you can to arrange your environment to get your needs met through the actions or requests that you make of other people. Being dependent on others to meet your needs creates hurt and disappointment, and it denies your own capabilities and resources to get your needs met.

Here's a beginning list of individual's needs:

- To feel loved unconditionally by at least a few people
- To get recognition for your accomplishments
- To be touched, hugged, or kissed affectionately
- To be listened to, heard, and supported
- To be forgiven when you do something wrong

If you identified any of these as your own unmet needs, what are some action steps that you can take to have that need be met? Who can help you with this? By what target date will you make that change? Take some time to think through this and make a list (for yourself) of actions dates and possible consequences of getting these needs met.

Successful and healthy relationships expect that each partner invest some of their time and energy into satisfying the needs and desires of their partner.

If these relationship needs are not being met satisfactorily, the relationship is in serious trouble and eventually may break. Each partner should take some action for satisfying needs apart from the relationship. Now, how about your partner's needs? Here are some conversations to have with your partner that will give you a great understanding of your partner's needs, as well as your own for the relationship:

1. What needs and desires do you expect your relationship to meet?

2. What are your partner's needs (as you understand them) that they expect the relationship to meet?

3. What are you willing to do to meet your partner's needs?

4. What is your partner willing to do to meet your needs?

"We all have different desires and needs, but if we don't discover what we want for ourselves and what we stand for, we will live passively and unfulfilled."
~ Unknown

For Women Only

Speaking of needs, let's talk about one of the most argued-about needs between a couple: sex and marriage. They do go together, don't they? No. There are many sexless and low-sex marriages today, and if I take stock of the clients in my office, the number of marriages that have infrequent or no sex is increasing. According to some studies, this is not a phenomenon. In a 2005 *Family Circle* national survey, 21% of married women considered their sex lives to be boring and routine, 21% reported that they had no sex life at all, and almost 50% reported no desire to have sex with their partner. And remember: These are only the women that responded; there are many, many more out there that seem to feel the same way.

Women access distinct parts of the brains for multitasking, whereas men generally focus on one thing before moving on to the next. Women need a transition time of about 10 to 30 minutes between activities, so turn off the TV and take a sensual time-out before you even hit the sack.

Having sex can be like going to the gym: Your mind and body rebel against it, but once you've done it, you feel amazing. The standard wisdom says a woman's sexual cycle moves from desire to arousal to orgasm. For women in long-term relationships, desire often comes after arousal. So instead of listening to the little voice that whispers it's time to sleep, be receptive to your partner's touch.

Where are all the sexually confident women—and why have they disappeared? As single women, we had our confidence, style, longing, and attraction. We worked for years to find the groove that would bring us sexual fulfillment and everlasting desire. Many of my female clients considered themselves to be a sexual goddess in their single lives. What has created the changes that are occurring in the American marriage?

Sleeping next to the same partner night after night, and wondering where desire has gone and if it will ever return, many women (and men) may give up and decide that their unfulfilling sex life is the norm—the price paid for security and stability in a relationship. Your partner is no longer pursuing you as they did when you were dating; you feel that your body is ugly from childbirth or aging; the sexual routine that you have fallen into is as dry and tasteless as an old piece of toast. Where's the butter?!

There are many reasons that women have lost their sexual confidence. Let's explore two of the key issues: your body and your mind. After all, who can feel beautiful with a post-partum body, complete with stretch marks, a flabby tummy and a chest that has gone south? Many women use excess food as their drug of choice to medicate these feelings of emotional pain, comparing themselves to the air-brushed models that are everywhere. Let me tell you something that I am 99% sure of—because of working with hundreds of couples and knowing the male perspective: Men *do not care* about your post-partum body. What they *do* care about is your sexual expression. Men are attracted to women who are sexually confident with themselves—not the way your body looks. So, turn off the lights, light a candle, and know that your husband wants to be there with *you,* not an air-brushed model.

How about your mind? Many women who have families, work full-time, and maybe even go to school are simply exhausted at the end of the day. If your idea of a blissful evening is Chinese takeout, paper plates, and being in bed at 8 p.m., you are not alone. We can let our minds rob us of sexual confidence, or we can find some other ways of making it work for us and finding the energy and desire again. No doubt about it, finding time for sexual expression while having a family is difficult, but not impossible. Look at your schedule. Yes, I know that it's busy, but there is *somewhere* in that schedule where you can devote 15–20 minutes to your husband, and to yourself. Don't you both have to take a shower in the morning?

What a good bonding opportunity—and you can find others at mid-day, creating a lunchtime rendezvous with your partner that will make the rest of the afternoon go by in a flash. If you are an evening person, just make sure that you leave some time for each other before you run out of gas.

Marriage is hard work, and so is keeping your sexual confidence. Remember to butter that toast in the morning!

'T' Is for Trust

"When mistrust comes in, love goes out."
~ Irish Saying

Becoming mistrustful of everyone around us is harmful. It limits the strength and number of our social connections, and may leave us isolated from the rest of the world. It is critical to learn how to rebuild trust, even if you feel like your relationship has been destroyed. Trust is not just essential to relationships; it is the cornerstone of a happy, healthy life.

As a couple's therapist, I have observed that the most important predictor of rebuilding trust in a relationship is the ability of both partners to take responsibility for what happened. This can be incredibly difficult if you are the betrayed partner. But it is a crucial step to saving the relationship—and laying the groundwork for reducing the probability of a repeat event.

After establishing mutual responsibility, the next step is to re-gain a sense of control. This is based on the idea that we are not victims, at the whim of our partner's actions or of our own mistakes. We *do* have control over our actions and thoughts, and can make decisions to improve our relationships. Whatever action you take, it is important to heal the wounds of the past.

How do you rebuild trust when you have lost it?

1. **Turn it off.**

    How many laptops, notebooks, smartphones, and big screens do you have in your home? All forms of media used in the extreme can isolate us and change our focus to the negative aspects of our society. We can build trust by communicating and discussing the issues with our partners, friends, and peers. Talking and conversing in person can drastically increase our sense of trust over an internet exchange.

2. **Get out.**

    Get out of the house, and meet a friend for coffee or your partner for lunch. Join a community group, organization, or interest group, or take a class. Organize block parties, garage sales, potlucks, or other neighborhood activities. This fosters social networks as well as trust. *Be* with other people!

The roots of trust are built in our childhood, where we learn to receive consistent, predictable care from our parents. Trust is built on order and predictability, which makes it even more psychologically traumatizing when that trust is broken. Many studies show that psychological traumas (like discovering an affair) can have an effect on brain functioning long after the event has actually happened. One of these common changes is the development of hyper-vigilance (think sleuthing) to prevent further assaults. Being hyper-vigilant is a survivor perspective; it protects us from harm.

These behaviors are commonly acted out by the partner who has been betrayed, by being looking for and being ultra-aware of *any* change in behavior or pattern from their partner. Unfortunately, being hyper-vigilant is non-discriminating. This puts us in a position to mistrust everyone around us: other family members, co-workers, community or spiritual leaders. This change in our perspective can be very harmful to our social connections. How can we prevent ourselves from mistrusting everyone around us after a betrayal?

Many levels of trust are built in, or foundational, that we take for granted. These levels of trust become more important when the higher level (betrayal) of trust has been broken. Identifying these lesser levels of trust is like trying to build a beautiful garden. You want the flowers to blossom, so that you can reap the rewards visually of the flowers in their color and beauty.

If they don't bloom, or bloom and then die, you may decide to give up your efforts to cultivate the flowers. But wait—what about the soil, the water, the sun—all the elements that are still there? These are the foundational pieces that are always there, no matter what. To ignore or give up on these pieces of the garden is to ignore the building blocks that are essential for growth.

How does this apply to your relationship? Let me ask you this: Do you "trust" your partner to pick up something from the store that they said they would? Do you "trust" them to pick you up when promised? Do you "trust" them to not steal your money and to not burn your house down? My point is this: Trust is a matter of degree. How can you learn to trust again? The fact is, you already do.

Both partners have a responsibility about restoring trust in a relationship. The person who broke the trust needs to genuinely do all they can to restore that trust. The other person needs to recognize that effort and ultimately forgive the other for past mistakes. You can't hold a mistake over someone's head forever, especially if the person is doing all they can to make things better. That will only lead to bitterness for both of you.

It happens to be our country's motto, but who else do we trust? Every-where we look, we see evidence of mistrust: in our governments, our communities, and our relationships. Trust is an intrinsic part of human nature; it's the basis of the healthy psychological development that usually develops between an infant and its caregiver. Trust is essential to healthy, strong relationships. How do we get it back?

Trust in others depends on face-to-face contact. Notice that I did not say Facebook. We are much more isolated today than previous generations were, and we have fewer close friends and organizations in which we are active.

The internet and TV are great communication tools, but they cannot be a substitution for personal interaction. These mediums are drains on our personal time that could be spent face to face with a friend, family member, or community member.

People trust people that they *know* before trusting a stranger, so the more people that you know, the more you will trust. Trust instills a feeling of good will between individuals and, in turn, benefits the community.

You can't expect your relationship to recover from trust issues in one day. Even if you are lucky and your partner agrees to forgive you, it does not mean that you won't have to continue to prove yourself. This process could even take years, but it all starts with the little things.

You can begin to build confidence from your partner by simply doing all the things you say you will. Showing up on time and following through on tasks may seem simple, but living up to even the smallest expectations will reflect well upon your intentions to save your relationship. Persistence and honesty are the two most important words in rebuilding trust. Reaffirm the commitment to the "garden" of the relationship by talking about shared goals and interests.

Action Step

5 Ways to Build Trust with Your Partner:

1. Make sure that you say what you mean, and mean what you say.

2. Keep your promises, even if you regret making the promise.

3. Be more predictable. Nothing will set off mistrust faster than sudden changes in the relationship or pattern.

4. Be open about changes that you are making. You won't be staying the same all the time; just let your partner know in advance.

5. Be an open book, with no secrets or suspicious behaviors. Your partner will reciprocate.

Our relationships are built upon the idea that we can trust those who we care about the most to behave in a consistent, reliable manner. When this belief is shattered, our emotions and common-sense dissolve and re-frame our reality. It feels like all that we have trusted in may not be as it appears. Let's look at one common area of trust breaking between partners: our social lives.

Social Calls

How do you know if your social life is helping or hurting your relationship? Our social lives are important; they allow us to have fun, relax, unwind, and get away with friends or family. What is crucial to our relationships is determining whether our social behaviors are authentic to who we are and what we are trying to achieve in our relationships. Many times, the two are out of sync. Here are some questions to ask yourself if your current social life seems to be blocking you from having a healthy relationship:

1. Do you revert back to adolescent behaviors in social situations, such as getting drunk, becoming obnoxious, or being sarcastic every time you are with a certain group of friends? Does this behavior help or hurt your current relationship? If you find yourself having a huge argument with your partner after every party or gathering, it might be time to re-evaluate your behaviors.

2. Do you hang out with people who are supportive of your relationships, or who are critical? Everyone needs good role models, especially when in a relationship. Spend time with people who are relationship- or marriage-friendly, not those who are a continual negative influence. The buddy that supports your drunken musings of wanting to cheat on your partner is not a good role model for your relationship—and your partner knows that, too.

3. Does your social life foster trust and integrity? This is a big one. If your actions are not trustworthy, how can you build trust in a relationship? As anyone who has lost the trust in a relationship can tell you, without trust the relationship will die or at the very least take a long time to recover. Make no mistake: Our social lives are a huge influence on our relationships. Don't get in your own way by keeping behaviors that no longer serve you. Be authentic in all your actions.

Scuba Lessons

Tonya and Randy had just experienced an "air leak" in their relationship. Randy had admitted to Tonya that he had been having thoughts of having an affair with someone. He had been very concerned when an opportunity had presented itself to cheat, but he had backed out at the last minute. Tonya was shocked, hurt, and relieved at the same time. Randy was confused about his emotions and guilt-ridden over how close he came to ruin their relationship. They had come to me to figure out what had gone wrong, what was missing in their relationship, and how to prevent an affair from happening in the future. The couple had been married for several years, had no children, and enjoyed their time with each other. How had they gotten to the point of nearly throwing away a good relationship?

This couple needed to understand how they went from happily married to a couple on the brink. What had happened was that, over the years, the trust had eroded in their relationship, leaving the two with feelings of being disconnected and alone. This gradual erosion occurred over seemingly inconsequential things, like being caught in a small white lie, hiding a piece of clothing or hunting equipment that had been purchased from each other, or omitting the full truth about an incident. While none of these trust-breakers was huge on its own, over the years they contributed to an environment within their marriage that didn't foster trust in each other. Working with this couple, I immediately saw that trust was one area that needed some attention quickly.

As we talked about their relationship, it became clear that they trusted each other implicitly in certain areas, and one of those was their mutual love of scuba diving. Randy and Tonya had taken hundreds of dives together, over several years of travel. They had trained extensively for their hobby, and when it came to diving, they trusted each other implicitly. We identified what needed to happen before, during, and after a dive that created their trust in each other, a trust that, if shaken, could impact their very lives.

Here is the plan what we created for Tonya and Randy that will prevent an "air leak" in the future.

☐ Plan the Dive, Dive the Plan

Tonya and Randy needed to plan ahead for trouble spots in their relationship. They needed to develop a warning system that would alert them to upcoming "danger zones," and stick to the plan that they had chosen. Deviating from their plan would not be allowed unless they mutually agreed.

☐ Buddy System

Just like in their dives, this couple had to be reliant on their partner to watch each other's back in dangerous waters, locate sharks in the ocean, and monitor equipment failure. They had to have complete confidence in each other's abilities to handle a crisis, and that they knew enough about each other to trust their actions.

☐ Signals

In the water, there is no conversation. How do you communicate when you are limited in what you can say? You come up with another language. Tonya and Randy had hand signals that they had created and agreed on prior to the dive—and used those signals to communicate to each other what was happening.

☐ When in Doubt, Just Get Out

When all else fails or in times of trouble, get out of the water. Tonya and Randy knew that in the case of dark waters, equipment failure, or sharks, it was time to get out of the water and regroup. No amount of training or knowledge can help when the waters are too dangerous. Realizing that you are not infallible is important in preventing affairs.

RSS Feed:

A buddy system in your relationship is essential to provide a consistent and trusting environment.

Action Step

Sit down for 15 minutes with your partner and discuss your buddy system. What signals do you give each other in times of trouble? What are the signals that you both agree on? How will you know if your partner is in trouble? Answering these questions will take you far when things are rough and cultivate the soil for your garden of trust.

'S' Is for SMART Goals

"The more intensely we feel about an idea or goal, the more assuredly the idea will direct us along the path to its fulfillment."

~ *Earl Nightingale*

Setting goals is essential to relationships. Without goals, we are setting sail in a rudderless boat, and embarking into shark-infested waters. Goals should be defined by both partners, be mutually agreed on, and have a schedule that both of you can count on. When creating a goal, look at this formula:

- ☐ S   Specific
- ☐ M   Measurable
- ☐ A   Action-oriented
- ☐ R   Realistic
- ☐ T   Time-limited

These elements are the crucial pieces that need to be a part of your goal for it to be achievable—and why would you want a goal to *not* be achievable? That would be setting yourself up for failure, and that doesn't help when you are trying to prevent an affair in your relationship.

Here are some examples from couples that I hear often: "I want to feel closer to my partner," "I feel like we are more roommates than lovers," "We don't have anything to talk about anymore; the relationship isn't what it used to be." These are "goals" that couples want help with, but they are more statements than goals. When you are looking to reconnect with your partner, think about how that actually *looks* in your head. Are you sitting at a table in a restaurant, looking into each other's eyes and having interesting conversation? Are you holding hands and watching a movie together, secure in the feeling that you don't necessarily have to speak to each other to connect? What are your visuals that occur when you are thinking about reconnecting with your partner? To have a SMART goal, you have to first visualize it in your mind.

Action Step

Relationship Review

Carrying out a "relationship review" allows you to identify the positives and negatives your relationship and look at areas that you might want to improve. Try to be honest with yourself and your relationship as you move through this exercise.

Positives and negatives can refer to you, your partner, or your relation-ship. Ideally all three areas should be looked at in order to get the best picture of what is currently going on in your relationship. One of your positives might be that you are a good listener, but a negative could be that you always have to win arguments. Potential is about the opportunities available to you to strengthen your relationship. For example, an opportunity could be that you are having a two-week holiday together, which will give you much needed personal time together. A concern is a threat that could harm your relationship—for example, an existing medical condition that could develop into illness.

Take a piece of paper and divide it into four parts. Write one of each of the four headings (Positives, Negatives, Potential, and Concerns) in each box.

Work through each box thinking about how they apply to you and you partner.

☐ With positives, do you have good communication in your relationship? Do you have a good sex life? Do you spend quality time together as a couple? Do you think about money in the same way?

☐ When thinking about negatives, consider this: Do you argue a lot? Do you flirt with other people? Do you push social boundaries when out in public, creating uncomfortable situations? Have you let your appearance and health go?

☐ When looking at potential think about this: How do you see yourself and your partner going into the future? Do you look forward to having an empty nest, your retirement, or traveling together? How much time will you spend together? Could you spend more time together now as a family? Could you develop a hobby together? Do you have common interests?

☐ Identify your concerns. Have you been unfaithful, or do you have frequent thoughts of being unfaithful? Have you or your partner's appearance or behavior radically changed? Do you have different views when it comes to commitment, money, sex, or children? Are there any threats of job loss? Do you have medical problems that could develop?

After you have finished the review, the final stage is to make a plan and decide what SMART goals you need to make. What change can you make that will result in a positive outcome for your relationship? Remember: Changes can be made quickly when you are motivated, and will have an immediate impact on the relationship. The SMART goal plan should give you an opportunity to celebrate the good things, to work on relationship and personal weaknesses, and to do your best to neutralize impending concerns. This proactive approach to your relationship helps you to keep your choices and actions on the straight and narrow, and creates more connection with your partner.

"One small step can change the course of your life."

~ Cheryl Richardson

The 5Cs Reconnection Plan

When the thrill is gone from the relationship, couples need guidelines to help reconnect, and I have a foolproof plan that will reconnect the two of you. There are five key areas of relationships gone south; these are the areas that need the most attention when reconnecting with your partner—and are proven to help you reconnect quickly. Here are the five keys for reconnecting with your partner:

- ☐ **Charisma**
- ☐ **Communication**
- ☐ **Caring**
- ☐ **Commitment**
- ☐ **Compromise**

I'll explain these terms, define them, and give you some action steps to improve these areas to quickly reconnect with your partner.

Charisma

I define charisma as meaning newness, uniqueness, and freshness. It shows your willingness to look at something from a new angle, perspective, or point of view. Are you continually open to fresh perspectives, unique experiences, or new interests? Many couples complain about how their relationship is not exciting anymore and that they never do anything fun. (When was the last time we…?) You get the idea. What are you doing about it? Think about the last time that you and your partner tried something different (a new restaurant, a concert, an outdoor event, a hike).

Many people have a problem with charisma because to them it means *change*.

For many, if you use the word *change* they immediately see this in their head:

change = pain = fear

Yes, there are those two words again: *pain* and *fear*. But change is not always painful. Change also means "to transform." Here's a new equation to think about:

change = transformation = growth

Make an effort to think about change as growth. Trying something new in your relationship creates a shared experience that neither of you are familiar with—which is what great stories are made of. This glides right into our next "C."

Communication

Communication should be simple, right? It sure was in the beginning of the relationship; you never had *enough* time to talk about everything that you wanted to talk about with your partner, spending countless hours on the phone having long conversations that took you into the middle of the night, just to do it again the next day. Remember when you couldn't wait to speak to your partner, to tell them every tiny detail that happened to you that day? Now, there are long, heavy silences and endless stretches of non-conversation, making you wonder how you ever filled up that time with before with meaningful conversation. That old cliché about the couple at the restaurant, never speaking to or looking at each other—is that secretly you and your partner? Or maybe it's not so secret; you realize that you and your partner have not conversed about anything beyond whose turn it was to take out the trash in years. Sounds like you might need a little small talk in your lives.

Going back to the first "C" of charisma, you can see how delving into new experiences can give you some good fodder for stories, which makes for some great small talk. Small talk has a bad reputation for only being useful at social events, like parties where you hardly know anyone. But if you think about it, small talk is what brought you and your partner together in the first place: talking about current events, music, religion, politics, philosophy, art, etc. These subjects initially connected you with each other and kept the connection going.

After couples have been together for a while, they slide into "shop talk." Shop talk can be defined as the logistics of what goes on in your daily life: children, work, chores, and events coming up. What time do I need to pick up the kids? Do we have any milk in the house? What do we need to work on this weekend? Etc. While these types of conversations are a necessary part of daily living, they shouldn't take over your life, as they do with many couples.

Again, balance is the key, and many couples admit that their communications scales are out of balance when it comes to small talk and shop talk. Some couples have confessed that their shop talk conversations make up almost 100% of their daily communications.

RSS Feed:
Charisma provides the difference between small talk and shop talk, and small talk is the lifeblood of your relationship. If charisma dies, so does the small talk, and the longevity of the relationship will then be in jeopardy.

Caring

This is a simple but often overlooked element of reconnecting with your partner: caring for yourself and caring for your partner. If you are not caring for yourself, it's a given that you are not caring for your partner either. Remember the flight attendant and the oxygen mask speech? You have heard this so many times you could recite it yourself. ("Please put on your mask first, *then* the mask on someone needing assistance.") If you don't help yourself, you can't help anyone else.

Have you taken care of yourself? Have the years of being in a relationship made you complacent? Are you overweight, burned out, and exhausted? If you answered yes to any of those, how does this translate into your partnership? Your partner's vision of you is a direct reflection of what you are projecting about yourself. What are they seeing?

One of the reasons that you get off track is that you are out of sync with your personal values, which is a direct hit to your caring potential. If you are not living in alliance with your values, it's difficult to care for yourself, and others. You feel angry, frustrated, and resentful, all because you conflict with what you really believe and how you find meaning.

- If you are exhausted, what value are you living up to
- If you are feeling burned out, are you living with your own values or the values of your work environment
- If you are overweight, how is that value serving you

RSS Feed:
Your most important relationship is with yourself. Care for yourself and you will automatically care for your partner.

Action Step

If you ask most people what their values are, they will give you a blank look. It's not something that we spend much time on, or we believe mistakenly that it's a silly question. To care for yourself is to know what rules you are living by, and knowing what values you have is essential to the rules. Try a values clarification exercise: Spend 15 minutes and write down 20 values that are important to you—no less. Think of terms like *family, independence, love, freedom, knowledge,* etc. After you have completed this, pretend that you are traveling and can fit only ten of those values in your suitcase. The suitcase will only hold so much, so what can you live without? Quickly cross off ten of the values that you just wrote, identifying which ones are non-essential. You have ten left. Now divide your list in half again. Be brutal; you can only keep five. You will be left with your top five values that should be driving your life—not the other way around.

Most people are very surprised with what's left on their value list—and are not living within their own rules that they have defined. Is this you? Are you protecting and supporting your own values? If you find that you are not, find some ways to bring your personal values in balance with the reality of your life, and your relationship will improve substantially. Take the top values that you identified and start using them to reconnect with yourself and your partner.

Commitment

The meaning of commitment seems pretty straightforward. You start to date, fall in love, agree to be exclusively committed, and get married. What the word *commitment* means to you may be different from your partner's definition, but for most people marriage become the great equalizer. Marriage means that you have made a commitment to yourself, your partner, your families, and your community that you will persevere as a couple through thick and thin. That's great on the front end, but what about after being together for a few years? Try on this meaning for commitment: How committed are you to saying no? Here's what I mean:

To be fully committed to your relationship, you need to be able to use the word *no,* liberally and often. Generally speaking, people are not very good at this, so you may have to practice. The point is that every time you say no, you are saying yes to more energy, more time, more opportunity, and more connection with your partner. All the obligations and responsibilities that you have that is *outside* of your relationship—be it the coaching that you do for the soccer team, the board position that you accepted, or the school function that you volunteered for—are endless time drains that interfere with your relationship.

You need to build a "wall of no," a filter that surrounds you and your partner in a protective sheath of being a couple. Notice that I said filter, not a titanium barrier. Picture a coffee filter. The right filter allows you to brew a perfect cup of coffee, right? A "no" filter allows you to make choices about who and what comes through the filter, and when.

Without this filter, you are not truly committed, in the sense of the word that really matters. *Saying* that you are committed is not the same as *being* committed, and commitment shows up as saying no.

RSS Feed:
Brew yourself the perfect relationship by choosing a filter for the two of you. Using the same type of filter daily makes a great cup of coffee.

Compromise

Compromise has a bad rap. When you think of compromise, you think of losing. You have to give up something to compromise, right? Wrong. In business-speak, compromise should be a win-win for both parties involved. In a romantic partnership, compromise means that you both get something out of the interaction. It shouldn't feel that you have to lose a piece of yourself or your needs in order to gain a solution.

Partnerships are all about compromise, so how can you do better? When you have a conversation or interaction with your partner, is about control, pride, or insecurity? Or are you fully present and engaged in finding a solution that works for both of you? Spend a bit of time thinking about this and see what you come up with. Go over the last few arguments that you've had with you partner to see where you could have said something or done something different that would have produced a better outcome. You should both feel *good* when the conversation is over—and that you have both *gained* something from the interaction. That's the true meaning of compromise.

Action Step
From You and Me to We

Here are some of the key issues that cause fighting with partners. Over the next few weeks, set aside some time to discuss these issues and reach an agreeable plan for the two of you. How will you handle the following?

Families of Origin

1. Holidays: How often will you visit? For how long? Do you go together or alone?
2. Phone calls: How often will you talk to parents, siblings, or other relatives on the phone? Will frequent calls disrupt your couple time or blend with your plan?
3. Intrusions: How will you handle family members who ask for too many personal details, offer too much advice, try to take over aspects of your life, or are a drain on your couple's time and energy?

Individual and Mutual Friends

1. How will you maintain friendships with people just one of you knows and enjoys?
2. How will you build a network of mutual friends, especially other couples?
3. How will you balance individual friendships with your need to socialize as a couple?

Spending some time on discussing these common topics will help to head off many arguments.

Healthy Habits

Okay, it's time to sum things up. You have your **5C's Plan for Reconnection,** your **RSS Feeds,** and several **Action Steps** to help prevent affairs in your marriages. Here are some final thoughts on doing everything you can to protect your marriage.

It's easy to pick up bad habits, and not so easy to form good ones. You can strengthen your resolve in preventing an affair in your marriage by creating some healthy habits to follow. Many people believe that it takes 30 days of daily action to form a new habit that will stick. Here are some healthy habits that will help protect your marriage:

Mentor Couples

Remember when we talked about your physical environment? Filling your surroundings with marriage-friendly people will support you when you are floundering, and celebrate with you when things are going well. Who better to share your marital challenges with than a mentor couple? Finding a mentor couple isn't difficult; just take a look around you. Look for a couple that has been married a long time, has withstood the ups and downs of marriage, and is still together. Try your social circles, your church, and your community. Couples that have been together for years will be happy to take you under their wing and mentor you; they have traveled the marriage road successfully and want to share their success with others. Mentor couples are a tremendous resource that can give you great benefits.

"I" Statements

1. During your evening meal together, avoid watching the television, reading the mail, or reading the newspaper. Look directly at your partner and have a conversation.
2. Ask open-ended questions to encourage your partner to open up and talk. Open-ended questions begin like this:
    a. Tell me about....

      b. What do you think of...?

      c. What was it like when...?

3. Check your communication with your partner and beware of using "you" messages. These are statements that begin with the word *you*. For example:

      d. You need to come home by 6:00.

      e. You shouldn't do that.

      f. You should call me if you are going to be late.

"You" messages are damaging because they make the other person feel bad or that they are being blamed. It feels like you are talking down to them and it can put them on the defensive.

If you want to demonstrate to your partner that you respect and care about them, try substituting "I" messages instead. When you start your statement with *I,* you are taking responsibility for the statement. "I" statements are less blaming and negative than "you" messages.

Try this formula:

your feelings + description of the behavior + effect on you

Here's how it would sound: "When I heard that you had to work this weekend, I was angry that you hadn't asked me first if I wanted to spend time with you."

It takes some practice at first, but with a little patience and time you will be communicating in a more positive way with your partner and building some healthy habits that will keep your pants on.

Now What?

"Even if you're on the right track, you'll get run over if you just sit there."

~ *Will Rogers*

You've finished the book. What should you do now?

RSS Feed:
Do something—now! Nobody ever sat their way to a successful relationship.

If you have spent your time reading the contents of the book without doing the exercises, here's what you should do next:

- Go back and do the action steps throughout the book.
- Read over all of the RSS Feeds again, and commit them to heart.
- Review the case studies to see where *you* fit into the picture.
- Spend a little time with yourself, and reflect on your perspectives of what you have read.
- Have a discussion with your partner about their ideas as well.
- **Take action now! Proactive always feels better than reactive.**

"Love is the master key which opens the gates of happiness."

~ Oliver Wendell Holmes

If All Else Fails

"Love is like a puzzle. When you're in love, all the pieces fit but when your heart gets broken, it takes a while to get everything back together."

~ *Unknown*

What if you have already had an affair? How do you work through this pain, make the important relationship decisions about fight or flight, and get back to some kind of normal?

Here's a bit about me: I am a psychotherapist that specializes in relationships, and the owner of Albuquerque Family Counseling. I work with couples who are trying to get through *really* difficult times in their relationships: sexual addictions, affairs, cheating, emotional infidelity—you get the idea. Over the years, I have helped *hundreds* of couples and individuals through some really bad times, and I can help you, too. The following tips, taken from my experience with couples, have been the most effective in moving through the experience of an affair.

Getting over an affair is not easy. This is a situation in which you thought that you would never find yourself. Now that you have found out about your partner's affair, what can you do to help:

- Stop the pain?
- Stop obsessing over the other woman or man?
- Pick up your crushed self-esteem and carry on?

Stop the Pain

First, please realize that going through an affair will take you on a course that is similar to the process of grief. You will pass through several different stages of emotion and pass through them more than once. You will need patience and commitment. Realize that you will never have your old relationship back; it was gone when the knowledge of the affair came to light. This is like mourning: the awareness that things will never be the same, and an acceptance of the event. What you need to think of for the future is what I call the "new normal." The new normal is about letting go of the idea that your life will ever be the same; it won't.

What *is* possible is that you can get through this and come out with an even better relationship, more self-esteem, and better communication—if you decide to. There is no standard amount of time to do this. Remember: You have been terribly hurt, shocked, and betrayed by someone close to you. Take your time! Don't feel the need to "get over it" on someone else's time table or pressure from your partner. Also, try not to make any hasty decisions at this time. Most importantly, let all of your emotions out. Talk to others who are supportive, journal your feelings, or write a letter to your partner. The progress will not be linear; you will have days where you feel like you have gone two steps forward and three steps back. This is normal, and you will heal with time and patience.

Stop Obsessing

This is really important: You *must* stop obsessing about the other woman (or man). I call this the "affair partner." I know that there are images going through your head that sometimes won't stop. I know that you want to constantly check your partner's cell phone, e-mails, texts, briefcase, and credit card bills, looking for information. You want to know about the other person: who they are, what they look like, what they wear, what they talk about, where they live, and how they could possibly have connected with your partner. Your mind is trying to fill in the details, but your mind does not know the difference between truth and reality. This can end up hurting you as much as the affair itself. You feel that you must have this information, and even though you may have good intentions about moving past this, you cannot seem to stop thinking about the person that was with your partner.

TRUTH: Every single person who has gone through the betrayal of an affair feels exactly as you do.

This is an endless loop of obsession that will not help you recover and heal.

One technique to help with this is the "obsession diet." Decide that you will only spend a set amount of time each day on thinking about the affair, say 30 minutes. Be diligent about this time, and do not let yourself go over the allotted time frame. Use a timer, and spend the time thinking about anything that you want with regard to the affair, but stop when the timer rings. This will help you to discipline yourself to "turn it off." Another technique is called "thought stopping." This means literally to "stop" the thought and use self-talk. Tell yourself "STOP" when the thought starts to come into your head. Continual practice will be very powerful to stop the obsessing.

The truth is it is not about the other person. There is nothing special about this person. People cheat because of how they feel about themselves—something that has nothing to do with you. Most studies show that the cheater stays in their primary relationship and has regretful feelings about the affair. They also admit that the person with whom they had the affair was not more attractive than their partner. *This is one of the hardest things to accept,* as we think that there must be something else that we could have done, should have done, or not done, in order to stop the affair from happening. All you really need to understand is why the affair happened, and how you can better yourself and your relationship as a result. Here's one more reason to stop the obsession: By giving into it, *you are giving away your power* to the other person. Don't spend one minute of mental energy on those thoughts. You and your relationship is what you need to think about.

TRUTH: The word *why* is not your friend.

Pick Up Your Self-Esteem and Carry On

Your self-esteem has taken a beating—a hard one. Probably, you feel worse about yourself than you can ever remember. Your thoughts of not being sexy enough, or attractive enough, or a good enough partner cause you to feel like you are "less than." Of course, this is not the case. If you let these feelings get out of hand, you will have a hard time climbing out of the self-confidence abyss.

The truth is, even if and when you have forgiven each other and want to move past the affair, the damage to your self-esteem can keep this from happening. It can be hard to believe your partner genuinely loves you, finds you desirable, and won't cheat again when deep down you are not sure of this yourself. You might fear there is something wrong with you or that your husband had an affair because of something the mistress or other woman had that you didn't.

So, this is the time to spend on you, someone that you have probably neglected for years. What are *your* needs? What will make *you* happy? Play up what you have; pamper yourself, get a facial, massage, make lists of positive traits that you possess, ask your friends and family what they love about you. Do anything and everything that will increase your self-confidence and put a smile back on your face. Begin to notice when someone flirts with you or sends you an admiring look, and realize that *you are still attractive*. One warning: Many people are tempted to go on out and have a "revenge affair." Doing this will only add to the mistrust, hurt, and pain that have already been caused. Although it may seem like a great way to get back at your partner, keep your integrity intact, and your self-esteem will follow.

Action Step

5 Ways to Start Building Your Self-Esteem

- Surround yourself with people who are positive and upbeat. Nothing is more draining than being around negative people.
- Commit to keeping a journal of your thoughts for two weeks. This journal is a place to jot down how you feel about yourself and what situations triggered these thoughts and feelings.
- Develop some positive statements about yourself that you know are true. Repeat these to yourself often.
- Try something new. The successful completion of new tasks and goals further increases self-confidence.

You've heard the saying "fake it till you make it." When you make up your mind to act like you have self-confidence, you are creating an environment for you to build self-confidence. Let it grow and flourish.

The Price of Forgiveness

No one gets through life without being hurt by another person. We all have experienced the pain of a thoughtless remark, gossip, or lie. If you have experienced an unhappy marriage or the devastation of infidelity, or suffered physical or emotional abuse, you know what it feels like to be hurt. It is tempting to hold on to these feelings and build a wall of safety around yourself, but the best way to heal is to forgive the person who hurt you.

But what is forgiveness, really? When you forgive another person, you no longer allow their behavior to cause you anger, pain, bitterness, or resentment. When you choose *not* to forgive, you make the choice to hold on to your feelings of resentment, anger, and pain.

Think of forgiveness as a gift that you give to yourself. It is *not* something you do for the person who hurt you. It is a gift to yourself, because it enables you to stop feeling painful feelings and pushing others away. Forgiveness frees you from anger, and allows you to restore your ability to have close and satisfying relationships with others.

Anger is a poisonous emotion that comes from being hurt. When you are consumed with anger and bitterness, it hurts *you* at least as much as it hurts the person who has harmed you. It is as if you are filled with poison. If these feelings are not resolved, they can begin to eat you up inside. You have two choices: to stay connected to the person who hurt you by keeping these poisonous feelings alive, or to let the feelings go and forgive the person who harmed you. When you withhold forgiveness, think about who is actually being hurt. It is more than likely that the person who is filled with anger and anxiety is you, not the other person.

Forgiving another does *not* mean you will never again feel the pain or remember the thing that hurt you. The hurtful experience will be in your memory forever. By forgiving, you are *not* pretending the hurtful behavior never happened. It *did* happen. The important thing is to learn from it while letting go of the painful feelings.

Forgiveness is *not* about right or wrong. It doesn't mean that the person's behavior was okay. You are not excusing their behavior or giving permission for the behavior to be repeated or continued.

Forgiveness can only take place because we have the ability to make choices. This ability is a gift that we can use whenever we wish. We have the choice to forgive or not to forgive. No other person can force us to do either.

One of the biggest reasons that it is hard to move past the affair is the fear that it will happen again, the fear of being "stupid," and the fear of more pain. I know that opening yourself up to being vulnerable and trusting again is really hard. Understanding how you and your partner got into this mess is the best line of defense that you have, and communication is crucial. Typical reasons for a partner's affair center on not feeling loved, understood, desirable, or appreciated anymore. How can you correct these feelings for *both* of you? If you are both committed to working on communication and relationship skills, the fix is easier than you think. And when both of you are feeling understood and appreciated, the chances of straying from the relationship are reduced. When this happens, the future looks pretty positive. This is the ultimate result: a new, fresh relationship free of doubt and full of hope. Amazingly enough, relationships *can* become even stronger after an affair. Don't ever doubt that you can get there!

www.ingramcontent.com/pod-product-compliance
Lightning Source LLC
LaVergne TN
LVHW051505070426
835507LV00022B/2926